FAMOUS LIVES

The Story of
GEORGE WASHINGTON
Quiet Hero

FAMOUS LIVES

titles in Large-Print Editions:

FAMOUS LIVES

The Story of
GEORGE WASHINGTON
Quiet Hero

By Joyce Milton
Illustrated By Tom LaPadula

Gareth Stevens Publishing
MILWAUKEE

For a free color catalog describing Gareth Stevens' list of high-quality books and
multimedia programs, call 1-800-542-2595 (USA) or 1-800-461-9120 (Canada).
Gareth Stevens Publishing's Fax: (414) 225-0377.
See our catalog, too, on the World Wide Web: http://gsinc.com

Library of Congress Cataloging-in-Publication Data

Milton, Joyce.
    The story of George Washington : quiet hero / by Joyce Milton ;
illustrated by Tom LaPadula.
        p. cm. — (Famous lives)
    Includes index.
    Summary: Recounts the life of America's first president, including
his youth in Virginia, military career, role in the formation of an
independent nation, and leadership of that new country.
    ISBN 0-8368-1469-X (lib. bdg.)
    1. Washington, George, 1732-1799—Juvenile literature. 2. Presidents—
United States—Biography—Juvenile literature. [1. Washington, George,
1732-1799. 2. Presidents.] I. LaPadula, Tom, ill. II. Title. III. Series:
Famous lives (Milwaukee, Wis.)
E312.66.M55   1996
973.4'1—dc20
[B]   95-53811

The events described in this book are true. They have been carefully researched and
excerpted from authentic biographies, writings, and commentaries. No part of this
biography has been fictionalized. To learn more about George Washington, refer to the
list of books and videos at the back of this book or ask your librarian to recommend other
fine books and videos.

First published in this edition in North America in 1996 by
Gareth Stevens Publishing
1555 North RiverCenter Drive, Suite 201
Milwaukee, Wisconsin 53212 USA

Original © 1988 by Parachute Press, Inc. as a Yearling Biography.
Published by arrangement with Bantam Doubleday Dell Books for Young Readers,
a division of Bantam Doubleday Dell Publishing Group, Inc.
Additional end matter © 1996 by Gareth Stevens, Inc.

The trademark Yearling® is registered in the U.S. Patent and Trademark Office.
The trademark Dell® is registered in the U.S. Patent and Trademark Office.

Printed in the United States of America

1 2 3 4 5 6 7 8 9 99 98 97 96

Contents

A Soldier in the King's Army

HERE HE COMES! HERE HE COMES AT LAST! This was the news young George Washington had been waiting to hear for days. His big brother Lawrence would be arriving before sundown.

Seven-year-old George had never met his big brother. Lawrence had been away at school in England for years. Ever since Lawrence wrote to say he was coming home, George's head had been full of questions. What would Lawrence be like? Would the two of them be good friends? How would it feel no longer being the oldest boy at home?

Now all questions were going to be answered. Excited and a little scared, George ran outside. There was a figure on horseback coming up the road. It was Lawrence! George had never seen anyone sit so straight in the saddle!

Lawrence leaped off his horse and ran to greet his family. The first thing George noticed was how tall his brother was. He was so tall that George had to bend over backward to get a look at his face. What he saw made him worry. Lawrence had a large nose and a long, sad face. He looked very serious. If George had been hoping for a new playmate, he was in for a disappointment. Lawrence was twenty years old and very grown up.

But nothing else about Lawrence was disappointing. In spite of his stern expression, he was kind and gentle. He loved to dance, play cards, and tell funny stories. He was one of the best riders George had ever seen. An expert shot, Lawrence knew all about guns and hunting. George soon decided that his brother was just about perfect, and he tried to copy everything Lawrence did.

Lawrence Washington was actually George's half brother. Lawrence's mother had died when he was just a little boy. After her death Lawrence and his brother, Augustine, were sent away to a school in England.

Lawrence's father, whose name was also Augustine Washington, soon married again. His second wife was named Mary. Together, they had five children. George, born in 1732, was the oldest son of this second family.

When George was a young boy, his family lived in a stone farmhouse near the Potomac River in Virginia. In those days Virginia still was a British colony. Even Virginians who had never been to England still thought of themselves as English. When they talked about going to England, they said they were going "home."

When Lawrence returned to Virginia, he told many wonderful stories about his stay in England. He talked about the big, crowded cities and the fine homes he had seen. And he talked about the glorious conquests of the British army. To a young boy growing up on a farm, it all sounded like another world.

But less than two years later, that other world came a little bit closer. The farmers in Virginia learned that England had declared war on Spain. Virginia was expected to send soldiers to fight in the British army. The governor of Virginia chose four captains to lead the troops. And the first captain he chose was Lawrence Washington!

Lawrence looked very grand in his new

uniform. George was extremely proud of him as he watched Lawrence riding at the head of his troops.

George decided that he wanted to go to school in England. Then he would become a soldier in the king of England's army. Just like Lawrence.

Into the Wilderness

ABOUT THE TIME THAT BROTHER Lawrence came home from England, the Washington family had moved to a new home—Ferry Farm, near the village of Fredericksburg, Virginia.

At Ferry Farm George spent long hours exploring out of doors. He became a good horseback rider, able to race across the countryside and jump fences. He went fishing and duck hunting.

There was a school in Fredricksburg. George may have attended classes there, but most of the time he did his lessons at home. One of his assignments was to copy out a list of 110 rules of good behavior. "Spit not in the fire" was one of them. Others were: "Sleep not when others speak"; "Wear not your clothes foul"; and "Be careful to keep your promise." The 110th was: "Be careful to keep alive in your breast that little spark of celestial fire called conscience."

When he was eleven years old, George went to visit some cousins who lived on a farm about forty miles away. He was enjoying having friends his own age to play with, so he stayed for a few weeks.

One day a rider appeared with an urgent message from home. Come home as soon as you can, the message said. Your father is very ill.

George saddled his horse and rode hard all the way back to Ferry Farm. But he was too late. His father was already dead.

Augustine Washington had been just forty-eight years old. His death was a shock to the whole family. For George, it meant that he would have to give up his plans for the future. His half brothers, Lawrence and Augustine, inherited most of their father's property. George, his mother, and the other children would still live at Ferry Farm. But they were not quite as well off as before. Going to England would not be possible, for his mother could not afford to send George away to school. And besides, she needed him at home to help take care of the farm.

He knew that it was now important to

have a way to earn money. One day he found some old surveying equipment in the barn. Surveying was important in Virginia. Farmers were constantly moving farther west and clearing new land. They needed surveyors to mark off the boundaries of their land. George had always been good at arithmetic. He began teaching himself to be a surveyor. He learned to look at soil and decide whether or not it was good for farming. Later, one of his jobs was laying out lots for the town of Alexandria, Virginia.

By now Lawrence Washington was living at Hunting Creek, the family farm that his father had left to him. The war with Spain was over, and Lawrence had been named commander of the Virginia volunteers. This was a very important position for such a young man.

After his father died, Lawrence changed the name of Hunting Creek Farm to Mount Vernon, in honor of an admiral he had served under in the war. He also decided that he could afford to get married. His bride was Anne Fairfax, a member of one of the most important families in Virginia.

Lawrence was doing very well, and George continued to admire and look up to him. He also loved Mount Vernon for something was always going on. Lawrence and Anne had many visitors. There were hunting parties and dinner parties. And the guests always seemed to have something interesting to talk about. They shared the latest news and their exciting plans for the future.

Some of these plans concerned George. Lawrence was always trying to think of ways to help his half brother. One of his ideas was that George should join the British navy.

George's mother did not like this at all. She refused to give her permission.

Mary Washington may have been right about the navy, but George was not happy at home at Ferry Farm. He and his mother did not get along. Maybe this was because Mrs. Washington wanted her son to remain a little boy for as long as possible.

One day, when George was sixteen, a letter from Lawrence arrived at Ferry Farm suggesting another sort of adventure. The Fairfax family had bought some land in the

Shenandoah Valley, a part of Virginia that was still wilderness. Anne's brother, George William Fairfax, was going with the surveyors to look over the new land. Did George want to go along?

He certainly did!

The Fairfaxes were a very wealthy, respected family, and the trip was going to last only a few weeks. This time Mrs. Washington did not try to keep George at home.

Day after day George and his friends rode west. Sometimes they would come upon a cabin built in a clearing in the forest. The owner would invite them to stay the night. They would spend the evening listening to stories about living in the woods alone, miles from the nearest neighbor.

Sometimes there were no cabins at all. The wooded hills seemed to go on forever. The surveyors were seeing places that no English settler had ever set eyes on before. They cooked their food over a campfire. At night they slept under the stars.

George and his companions had many adventures. Once they had to swim their horses across a fast-moving river. On another

leg of the journey, they switched to canoes and paddled forty miles in a single day.

One night some sparks from the campfire set their straw mattresses on fire. One of the men woke up, surrounded by smoke and flames. He screamed in panic and jumped to his feet. So did the others. They all danced around in the dark, stamping out the flames. Luckily, no one was hurt.

Another time the group ran out of food. They had been hoping to get dinner at a settler's cabin, but the cabin was not where they expected it to be. Some of the group went out with guns, hoping to shoot a bird or some game, but they did not catch anything. That night everyone went to bed hungry. George had been thinking of the trip as a great adventure. This experience made him realize how easily travelers in the wilderness could get into serious trouble.

Another day the surveyors met a group of thirty Indians. The Indians decided to hold a ceremonial dance. They made musical instruments right on the spot. One Indian made a rattle from a dried-out gourd. Another stretched a deerskin over a pot that was half full of water. The pot became a drum! George thought the dance was very exciting. He had never seen anything like it.

The trip lasted thirty-one days. When George returned home, Lawrence and Anne were eager to hear all about his adventures. Like the Fairfaxes, Lawrence was interested in buying land on the frontier. He and some friends had even started an organization called the Ohio Company, which planned to explore and trade in the new lands.

George had not gone far enough west to see the Ohio River. But he had already seen more of the frontier than many men twice his age. He had certainly seen more than Lawrence had.

After his Shenandoah trip Lawrence and his friends started to treat George like a grownup. He was still a teenager, but he was six-feet-two, as tall as Lawrence. George was a good athlete, and he had proved that he could survive in the wilderness. What's more, his quiet, serious ways made him seem older than his age.

*   *   *

George soon needed all his quiet strength because there was more trouble in the Washington family. Lawrence was ill. He coughed all the time. Every day he looked a little bit thinner.

George tried to think of ways to help Lawrence get better. First he took his brother to visit some hot springs in the Blue Ridge Mountains of northwestern Virginia. Bathing in hot springs was supposed to cure diseases. Lawrence did feel better for a while, but within a year, he was still very ill.

Next George took Lawrence on a trip to the Caribbean island of Barbados. Maybe the climate of a tropical island would work a miracle.

Barbados was beautiful, but George and Lawrence had nothing but trouble there. On their second day on the island, George woke up feeling hot and sweaty. Soon he had a high fever. He had caught smallpox, a very serious disease. George was ill for two whole months. He was lucky to recover at all. As soon as he felt strong enough, he returned to Virginia.

Lawrence stayed in the islands for a while.

But soon he, too, came home. His cough was not getting any better, and he missed his wife and home. A few months later he died.

George's idol and best friend was gone. But George didn't have time to feel sorry for himself. He had to take care of his brother's funeral. Then he set out to fill his brother's shoes. He became an officer of the Virginia volunteers, just as Lawrence had been. He even began to think about ways that he could make a success of his brother's plans for exploring the territory around the Ohio River.

A Narrow Escape

IN THE FALL OF 1753 GOVERNOR DINWID-
die of Virginia heard a rumor that made
him very unhappy. French soldiers were
moving south from Canada. The French had
already built several forts south of Lake Erie.
Now it looked as if they meant to go all the
way to the Ohio Valley, taking over lands
the Virginians wanted for themselves.

Governor Dinwiddie wrote to King
George II in England. The king sent back a
stern order. The governor was to send a message to the French soldiers: Get off our land,
or we will drive you out.

The governor and his friends were
pleased. They were happy to hear that their
king thought the Ohio lands were worth
fighting for. That left only one problem: The
message was sure to make the French angry.
Who would be willing to deliver it?

Governor Dinwiddie thought of George
Washington. George was only twenty-one

years old. But he knew the woods. He was tough, and he had good sense. The Fairfax family considered him very trustworthy.

George found a woodsman named Christopher Gist to be his guide. He also hired a Dutch settler named Jacob van Braam, who knew French and could be his translator. Last of all he hired four men who would take care of the horses and supplies.

It was already November when the seven travelers started out. The nights were cold. By day the sky was a silvery gray. In the mountains there was snow on the ground. The Indian trails were slippery with mud. The horses stumbled in the muck.

Finally the little group reached the Monongahela River. George decided to take a canoe and go on ahead. Soon he reached the place he had heard so much about—the Forks of the Ohio. This was the spot where the Monongahela and Allegheny rivers came together to form the Ohio River.

Starting from the Forks, it was possible to take a boat all the way to the Mississippi River. And from there a person could float all the way down the Mississippi to the Gulf of Mexico. Other rivers joined the Mississippi, too—rivers that came from the western part of North America, from lands that no English settler had ever explored.

Today the city of Pittsburgh stands at the Forks. But when George Washington saw the place for the first time, there was nothing—not even a single cabin.

Washington camped at the Forks for two days. He spent the time daydreaming about the fort that the Virginians would someday build on the spot. He even hiked up and down the riverbanks looking for the best place to build.

When Christopher Gist and the others arrived with the horses, the group moved on to an Indian village called Logstown. There George met the man the English called Half King. Half King was an important Indian leader. As you might guess from his name, Half King was not quite a king. But he was more important than an ordinary chief. He had the power to speak for a group of tribes called the Iroquois. The Iroquois were made up of six tribes who had taken sides with the English against the French. The English settlers called them the Six Nations.

Half King was very upset with the French for moving into his territory. He had been to see the commander of the French and made an angry speech. Now he repeated that speech word for word to George.

Half King had told the French: "If you had come in a peaceable Manner, like our Brothers, the *English,* we should not have been against your trading with us, as they do. BUT TO COME, FATHERS, AND BUILD HOUSES UPON OUR LAND, AND TO TAKE IT BY FORCE, IS WHAT WE CANNOT SUBMIT TO."

Half King's speech must have worried George. He wrote every word of it in his diary, and he wrote the part about building houses in capital letters. George knew very well that the English also wanted to build houses on Indian lands. But this was not a good time to discuss this with Half King.

George did not feel especially guilty about wanting to take the Indians' land. Like most English settlers, he thought that land ought to belong to the people who were able to put it to the most use, by clearing farmland and building towns and cities. Thousands of square miles of forestlands were in the western territories—and only a few thousand Indians. From the colonists' point of view, it wasn't fair that a few people could control so much land that was used for nothing but hunting.

Still, Half King's speech gave George a lot to think about. Half King was not stupid. No doubt he knew that the English and the French both wanted the same thing. So far the Six Nations had been loyal friends of the English. That hadn't changed. But George could see that it would not be a good idea to take the Indians' friendship for granted.

Half King and two other chiefs agreed to lead George and his men to the French forts. At the first fort they came to, the French pretended to be very friendly. They even invited George to have dinner with them.

At the dinner table the French officers laughed and joked. And while they laughed, they kept reaching over to pour more wine into George's glass. They knew that George was just a young man, and they were trying to get him drunk. Then maybe he would tell them all about the secret plans of the Virginians.

George smiled across the table at his hosts. He laughed at their jokes. Every time they proposed a toast, he raised his glass high in the air. But he just pretended to drink. Soon it was the French who were drunk. They boasted about how the French were going to take over the entire Ohio Valley. George remembered every word they said, and wrote them down in his diary. Now he knew the secrets of the French.

Later the French officers tried the same trick on the Indians. They gave Half King and the other chiefs a whole keg of brandy. The French hoped the Indians would get too drunk to travel. The trick didn't work with Half King either. The next morning he and the other Indians were up early, ready to travel on.

On December 11 George reached the fort where he was to deliver his letter. He put on the dress uniform that he had carried with him from Virginia. Standing very tall and straight, he presented Governor Dinwiddie's letter to the old French commander.

The commander sat down and wrote out his answer: The French had no intention of going back to Canada.

That meant war! George knew that he'd better hurry home with the French commander's reply. He wanted to warn the governor as soon as possible.

The French were still being very polite. But they kept thinking of excuses for preventing George and his companions from starting their journey home. Winter was setting in. The rivers were freezing over. Every day the Virginians delayed, the more dangerous their trip was sure to be.

Finally the French were able to talk Half King and the other chiefs into staying with them. George and his group would have to find their way back alone. By now it was also too late to make any speed on horseback. The ice on the trails cut into the horses' feet and legs and made them bleed. The horses could only go a few miles each day.

George and Christopher Gist decided to leave the other men with the horses and hurry on ahead.

George noticed how practical the Indians'

clothes were. Some Indians gave him a leather shirt and leather leggings to wear. Then he and Gist started hiking through the woods. That first day they walked eighteen miles. Christopher Gist did not think this was very far, but it seemed a long way to George. He was used to going everywhere on horseback. His feet were wet and aching from the cold.

The next day the travelers reached an Indian village. One of the Indian braves acted very friendly. He offered to show them a shortcut through the forest.

The three of them left the trail and started to hike through the snow. They covered about ten miles very quickly. George wanted to stop and rest. But the Indian refused. He warned that there were other Indians in the woods, unfriendly ones who were waiting to attack them.

Let me carry your gun, he told George. Then you will be able to walk a little faster.

George said, "No, thanks." He gritted his teeth and walked as fast as he could.

Gist was beginning to get suspicious. "How far is it to the next cabin?" he asked.

As far away as the sound of a gun firing, said the Indian.

They hiked on a little farther. By now Gist was really worried. He had a lot of experience at finding his way in the woods. He could tell they were walking north—the wrong direction.

Once again Gist asked the Indian how far they had to go.

As far away as the sound of two war whoops, said the Indian.

There wasn't much that Christopher and George could do. The Indian had taken them so far from the trail that they were completely lost. So they hiked on a few more miles.

Suddenly they came to a clearing in the forest. The woods had been dark and gloomy. But in the clearing the light was very bright. The sun sparkled on the fresh white snow.

George stopped to catch his breath. Then he realized that the Indian guide was no longer beside him. He had run ahead into the clearing.

All at once the Indian turned around and

fired his rifle. The shot cracked in the freezing air. George's eyes were so used to the gloom that the bright sunlight was almost blinding. For a few seconds he was completely confused. He couldn't see Christopher Gist anywhere.

"Are you shot?" he cried out.

"No!" Gist shouted back.

Both of them ran toward the Indian. They caught him as he was trying to reload his rifle. Now they knew that the Indian had been planning to rob them all along. Gist wanted to kill the man on the spot. But George wouldn't allow that. He had never killed anyone in his life.

When the Indian realized that the two Virginians weren't going to kill him, he ran off into the forest. George and Gist decided they had better get out of the area as fast as possible. Checking their compass, they headed in a direction that they thought must lead to the Allegheny River. They walked until late at night. And all the next day, too.

Finally they reached the banks of the river. There they tied some logs together to make a raft. Guiding the raft with poles made from tree branches, they started out. They had to steer around big chunks of ice. Once George lost his balance and fell in the freezing water. After a little while they came to a place where the river was frozen solid. They had no other choice but to leave the raft behind and walk.

That night they reached a trading post, where they could eat and sleep in a dry place. Best of all they could buy horses. The rest of the journey seemed almost easy.

Two weeks after New Year's, 1754, George was back in Williamsburg, the capital of Virginia.

The Virginians welcomed George as a hero. He had brought the French message back in just one month and five days. Everyone thought this was very fast for news to travel through the forest, especially in the middle of winter. The Virginians were sure that George's speedy return would give them a head start in getting ready to fight the French.

At War with the French

GOVERNOR DINWIDDIE SOON REWARDED George Washington by making him a lieutenant colonel. Only twenty-two years old, George was already second in command of the Virginia volunteers.

When spring came, the man who was first in command turned out to be too ill to lead an army through the wilderness. So Washington was put in charge of the first expedition against the French.

The Virginia volunteers were not a very impressive army. They had only one hundred fifty-nine men and a few wagons. They had no uniforms and very little food. The soldiers had to cut down trees and clear a road for the wagons as they went. It was slow, backbreaking work.

When the army reached Half King's territory, there was bad news. The French had already built a fort at the Forks of the Ohio, on the very spot where George had camped a few months before. Some Indian tribes had already gone over to the French side. What's more, Half King warned, there were French soldiers marching in the woods. One of Half King's braves had tracked their footsteps in the snow.

Washington decided to find the French before they found him. His little army sneaked through the woods and surrounded the French camp. The French soldiers saw they were caught and ran for their guns. Shots rang out! The war between the French and the English had begun!

When the excitement was over, the French officer in charge was lying dead on the field. George Washington had won the first real fight of the war.

Washington thought he had done well to catch the French by surprise. He wrote a letter to his younger brother Jack. "I heard the bullets whistle," he said. "And, believe me, there is something charming in the sound."

Later Washington's letter was printed in an English magazine. When King George II read it, he shook his head. He predicted that the young Colonel from Virginia would soon change his mind. Bullets lost their charm once you'd heard a lot of them.

In the meantime the French were saying that the Virginians had broken the rules of war. The French claimed they had been on a peaceful mission. They accused Washington's army of attacking them for no reason at all. Washington didn't believe the French story. But he knew that some people would.

Washington retreated to a meadow just south of the battleground. The Virginians worked fast to build a little fort. They called it Fort Necessity.

Only two hundred more soldiers arrived from Virginia—not enough men to fight the French. Washington decided it was time to call on the Indians of the Six Nations for help.

Very few Indians showed up. Many of the Indians had already decided that the French were going to win the war. The Virginians' army was too small. Colonel Washington was too young and inexperienced. Even Half King and his soldiers packed their belongings and left the area.

Only July 3 the French army arrived. This

time—just as King George had said—Colonel Washington did *not* find the sound of bullets whizzing all around him the least bit "charming." The shooting went on for hours. Soon over one hundred Virginians were dead. Washington had to surrender.

George Washington knew what it was like to come home a hero. Now he learned how it felt to be a failure. The worst blow of all was learning that he was going to be demoted to captain. He thought this was so unfair that he decided to resign instead.

George did not stay away from the army very long.

Early the next year the King of England decided to send one of his best generals to Virginia. Edward Braddock was an experienced soldier. He and his British officers wore handsome red uniforms. They knew how to drill and march in formation. And they had brought some shiny new cannons with them from England.

General Braddock soon heard that no one knew as much about the woods as George Washington. He offered to make Washington his personal aide. It was too good an offer for George to refuse.

Washington tried to tell the general what wilderness fighting was like. The French woodsmen and the Indians would try to catch them by surprise. Then they would disappear into the woods.

Braddock was not worried at all. "Regularity! Discipline!" These were his favorite words. He was sure his well-trained soldiers could beat a bunch of wild savages.

A few miles from the Forks of the Ohio, General Braddock's army met the French for the first time. When the shooting started, the English soldiers formed straight lines and stood there firing at the enemy. Their bright red uniforms made wonderful targets. The French and their Indian allies hid behind trees and picked the British off one by one. General Braddock was one of the first to get shot.

Washington tried to save the day. He rode around urging the soldiers to stay put. A bullet darted straight through his hat. Two more bullets burned holes in his uniform. Twice he had horses shot out from under him. Finally Washington was able to carry the general to safety, but it was too late. Braddock died a few days later.

It was another terrible defeat.

The English blamed the Virginians. They thought Virginia hadn't brought enough supplies for the war. They blamed the Virginians for giving General Braddock bad advice. They even claimed that the volunteers had panicked during the battle.

The Virginians refused to take the blame. They knew it had been the other way around—it was the British who had panicked. Braddock's defeat was partly just bad luck, but it showed the Virginians that the British army was not unbeatable after all.

After the battle Governor Dinwiddie offered to make George Washington a colonel again. Eventually Washington became the commander of all the Virginia troops in the war.

Colonel Washington remained a soldier for three more years. In 1758 the Virginians joined another British officer, General Forbes, in a new attack on the French. This time the Virginia volunteers wore leather

clothes and fought frontier-style.

Forbes's army reached the Forks of the Ohio on Christmas Day. Nothing but a pile of burned logs was left of the French fort. When the French heard Forbes was coming, they had decided to give up. They set fire to their own fort and ran away. The Ohio Valley would belong to the English settlers after all.

Mount Vernon

WHEN GEORGE WAS AWAY FIGHTING the French, he wrote long letters to his neighbor Sally Fairfax. In one of them he made a confession. He told Sally that he was in love. And, he added: "This Lady is known to you."

Did Sally Fairfax guess that she was the lady George Washington loved?

Probably she did. But she tried to pretend that she didn't understand his hints. Sally Fairfax was already married. Her husband was George Washington's best friend, George Fairfax.

As long as he was always away at war, George's crush on his pretty neighbor did no one any harm. But by 1758 the war with the French was coming to an end. George started to think about getting married. The time had come to forget about Sally.

When he was younger, George had been shy around girls. He wrote love poems in secret. But when the girls he liked were around, he never knew the right things to say. When he was twenty years old, he had finally worked up the courage to propose to a girl he admired, sixteen-year-old Betsy Fauntleroy. Betsy turned him down. And when he proposed again, she said no a second time. Now he was twenty-six years old and a war hero. But inside, he probably did not feel any more confident than he had years ago.

In the spring of 1758 one of George Washington's friends introduced him to Martha Dandridge Custis. Martha was only five feet tall—more than a foot shorter than George was. She had tiny hands and feet and shining dark hair. Although she was about George's age, she was already a widow. Her husband had died and left her alone with two children—a boy called Jack, and a girl called Martha after her mother, but nicknamed Patsy. Martha Custis also happened to be rich. Because of this, quite a few men were interested in marrying her.

George set his heart on winning the love of a woman who was considered the "best catch" in all of Virginia. This time he succeeded. Martha Custis was cheerful and easy to talk to. She was also grown-up enough to see that Colonel Washington would make a good husband.

They were married in January of 1759. Martha wore a white silk dress and shoes with diamond buckles. George wore a blue suit with a red silk lining. His red hair was whitened with powder. Powdered hair was considered very stylish.

George and Martha made their home at Mount Vernon.

A few years earlier Lawrence's widow, Anne, had remarried. Since she wanted to live in the house of her new husband, she agreed to rent Mount Vernon to George. During the years when he was fighting the French, George had very little time to spend at Mount Vernon. But after he met Martha, he began to think about turning the farm into a real home. He had a second floor built onto the little farmhouse. When he married, the house was ready for his new family.

George and Martha loved children. They wanted a large family, but they were never able to have any more children. This was very disappointing for them.

The Washingtons made up for their disappointment by paying as much attention as possible to Martha's two children. They were a very close family. Unfortunately, they also had more than their share of troubles.

Martha's little girl, Patsy, had a disease called epilepsy. Today epilepsy can be treated with medicines. In those days the doctors did not know how to treat it. Some of the treatments they ordered were nasty. The doctors had the idea that bleeding would wash the sickness out of a person's body. So Patsy had to sit still while they drew blood from her veins. She had to swallow horrible-tasting medicines. She spent days at a time in a darkened room. One doctor thought that Patsy might be cured if she wore a special ring made of iron. The Washingtons were so eager for Patsy to get better that they tried everything the doctors suggested. Patsy was very brave.

George Washington tried to make his

stepdaughter's life as happy as possible. Every year he ordered new clothes and toys sent from England. Once he gave Patsy a beautiful music box. Another year her special gift was a talking parrot. The Washingtons even invited a girl Patsy's age to live at Mount Vernon so their daughter wouldn't be lonely.

Patsy grew up to be a thin, frail teenager. Even though they could see that Patsy was not getting any better, her parents never gave up hope. Unfortunately, there was no happy ending to Patsy's troubles. She died when she was just seventeen years old.

Jack Custis was a different sort of problem. As a boy, Jack always managed to find some way of avoiding doing schoolwork. When he was older, he spent most of his time at dances and the racetrack. Some of Jack's teachers thought he would be better off if his mother and stepfather were more strict with him. But Martha spoiled her son terribly. And although George Washington could be stern when it came to disciplining his troops, he could never say no to his stepson.

When he was nineteen, Jack decided to

quit school and get married. Once again George found it impossible to deny Jack what he wanted. Perhaps he hoped that once Jack had a wife, he would become more responsible. But "Jackie" Custis never changed. He was a worry to his parents all his life.

In spite of these family troubles, there were many happy times at Mount Vernon. George loved being out of doors. He spent most of every day on horseback, riding from one of his farms to the next to see how the work was going. In the evenings he and Martha would dance and play cards. Almost every night they had guests for dinner.

Colonel Washington was said to be the best horseback rider in Virginia. He also had a reputation for being very strong. One of the many stories told about him was that he was so strong he could bend iron nails with his bare hands. No doubt some of these stories were exaggerated. But not all:

Once, some young men who were guests at Mount Vernon were playing a game. The object was to throw a heavy log as far as possible. When their host came along, they invited him to take a turn at the game. George acted reluctant. He wondered aloud if he could still keep up with the younger men. On his first try he pitched the log farther than any of them had all day.

Between them George and Martha Washington owned many acres of land, divided among several farms. Mount Vernon alone was like a miniature city. There were workshops for spinning cotton into cloth, and other workshops for sewing the cloth into dresses, shirts, and trousers. Barrels, tools, and wagon wheels were also made on the farm. The Washingtons even had a mill for grinding wheat into flour. Just watching over the farms and keeping their accounts was enough to keep one man very busy.

But of course, the hardest labor on the farms was done by black slaves.

George Washington often said that slavery was a bad system. He thought the slaves should be educated, so that when they became free they would have some control over their own destinies. At one time or another he discussed various plans for ending slavery altogether. He also hoped that the original

Americans, the Indians, would take up farming so that they could hold on to at least some of their valuable land.

Looking back on Washington's life, some people have been disappointed that he did not do more to put his ideas into practice. Like so many others, he found it easy to recognize injustice but hard to imagine how the world could ever be changed for the better.

In fact, no one enjoyed change less than George Washington. He loved Mount Vernon, and he loved being a gentleman farmer. After he left the British army, he considered his career as a soldier finished. His greatest ambition was to spend the rest of his life right where he was.

And for seventeen peaceful years that is exactly what he did.

Away from Mount Vernon, those years were not quite so peaceful. Ever since the war with the French ended, the American colonists had been losing faith in England. The colonists had done much of the fighting. But it was the English who decided the peace terms. The Americans who fought in the

French and Indian War had been promised land. Later the English changed their minds.

In all of the colonies there was trouble over taxes. The American colonists didn't feel they owed England anything. Why should they pay taxes when they had nothing to say about how the money would be spent?

The colonists felt that they were being treated like naughty children. The English parliament wasn't interested in hearing what the Americans had to say. It kept passing new taxes and thinking up ways to punish the Americans for not paying them.

A group called the Sons of Liberty started to organize parades and rallies against England. Sometimes they held mock trials of English politicians. The Sons of Liberty were especially strong in Boston. The English sent soldiers to Boston to make the people behave, but this just made the trouble worse. The soldiers acted as if Boston were a conquered city. Some of them stole food and insulted people on the street.

Even the little things the soldiers did drove the people of Boston half crazy: When the British army bands marched on parade, they loved to tease the Americans by playing "Yankee Doodle." This was the Americans' special song, and the British soldiers were always finding new ways to make fun of it.

In 1773 the English parliament put a tax on tea. That December the first three ships loaded with tea sailed into Boston Harbor. A few nights later about fifty Bostonians dressed up as "Indians." They smeared paint on their faces. They wore old blankets and put feathers in their hair. When night came, the "Indians" went on the prowl. They boarded the ships and threw all the tea into the harbor—about ninety thousand pounds of it!

This was called the Boston Tea Party.

The Sons of Liberty thought this was a good joke. But the English weren't laughing. A law was passed in London, closing Boston harbor. This put many people in Boston out of work. England also sent more troops.

In 1774 representatives from each colony decided to get together to talk about their troubles. This meeting, called the Continental Congress, was held in Philadelphia,

Pennsylvania. Virginia was allowed to send seven delegates. One of them was George Washington.

Philadelphia was humming with excitement. No one was sure how holding a congress was going to resolve their problems with England. But the delegates were proud of themselves for having the courage to speak up. Most of them had arrived with long speeches in their pockets. Everyone was talking and arguing.

Washington did not have much to say. He wasn't a speech maker. He just watched and listened.

But he was noticed. All the delegates had heard about Washington's adventures fighting the French. They knew that his first trip to the Ohio had been back in 1753—twenty-one years ago. Some of the delegates had been little children then. They expected Colonel Washington to be an old man. They were surprised to learn that he was just forty-two years old.

In the end the congress decided to send a message to King George III and the people of England. All they wanted, the delegates said, was their rights as Englishmen. They asked the king for justice.

The delegates' message was sent to England on the next ship. Then everyone went home to wait for the king's answer. They agreed to meet again on May 10, 1775.

Washington spent a quiet winter at home at Mount Vernon. Before he returned to Philadelphia, he heard some important news: The British commander in Boston had learned that the Massachusetts volunteers were hiding guns outside the city, in the towns of Lexington and Concord. He decided to send some of his soldiers to find the guns and take them away. The British troops—the redcoats, as they were called—left Boston on the night of April 18. They reached Lexington at four-thirty the next morning.

The redcoats expected to find everyone asleep. They didn't know that Paul Revere had already warned the town. About 130 men with guns were standing in the town square.

"Lay down your arms!" the British major shouted.

Neither side knew what to do. For a few minutes everyone just milled around. Then someone fired his gun. Soon everyone was shooting. Within minutes eight Americans were dead.

Did this mean war? People in Massachusetts certainly thought so.

Some people in the other colonies weren't sure. They thought the volunteers in Massachusetts were hotheads. But Washington took their side. People could only be pushed so far without fighting back, he said. The British were "trampling on the valuable rights of Americans."

When Washington arrived in Philadelphia for the meeting of the Second Continental Congress he was wearing his old army uniform.

That uniform said more than a hundred speeches. The delegates made up their minds that the time had come to fight for freedom. On June 15 they took a vote to decide who would command the American army. There was only one nomination: George Washington.

1776

BOOM! BOOM! BOOM!

For the third night in a row the Americans were firing off their big guns. The guns made a lot of noise. But they were not doing much damage.

Across the bay in Boston the British officers were having supper. Last night and the night before they had wondered what all the fuss was about. Now they simply shook their heads and kept on eating. They thought the Americans were foolish to waste so much gunpowder.

The British felt safe in Boston. Even though the American army was gathered across Back Bay in Cambridge, the British did not expect them to attack. The firing of the big American guns kept the British soldiers from riding out of the city to have a look around. But this did not really bother them. It was early March 1776, and the British leader, General Howe, had no plans to go anywhere until the weather was warmer.

So that night the British went to bed as usual. They weren't going to let the crazy Yankees ruin their sleep.

In the American camp no one was sleeping. As soon as the moon came up, lines of soldiers began filing out of camp. They were heading for the hills of Dorchester Heights, part of a long neck of land that stuck out into the bay right across from Boston.

Some of the soldiers carried rifles. Many more carried axes and shovels. Others drove wagons. The wagons were loaded with bales of hay and barrels full of stones.

All night long the soldiers worked. They dug trenches and cut down trees. They used wood and dirt to build walls that would protect them and their weapons. They set up the barrels so they could dump stones down on anyone who tried to climb up the hills to attack them.

In the meantime, more Americans were bringing cannons up the hill. The cannons were loaded on wooden sleds and wagons. Horses and men had to pull together to get them up the steep slopes. It was hard work, but everyone was moving as quickly as possible.

Sometimes the soldiers would look up and see a tall man on horseback watching over them. This, they knew, was their commander, George Washington.

Washington seemed to be everywhere. He would stop in one place just long enough to remind the soldiers to be very quiet. Boston was below them, just across the water. It was important not to make any noise that would warn the enemy.

When the British officers woke up the next morning, they got a big surprise. The American cannons were on top of Dorchester Heights—and they were pointing directly at Boston! It had all happened so fast, it seemed like magic. One British officer said that the work must have been done by the genie "from Aladdin's wonderful lamp."

Across the water George Washington waited. He was hoping that the British would send soldiers over to attack the Heights right away. Then he planned to sneak the rest of his army into Boston. With luck and hard fighting, the war would be over in a few days.

But the weather was not on Washington's side. That night a fierce storm blew in from the ocean. There was no hope of moving an army across the water in small boats.

A few days later it was the Americans' turn to be surprised. Early in the morning the bay was filled with boats. But Boston itself seemed very quiet. So did the British fort on Bunker Hill. A few brave American soldiers crept closer to the fort. At first they wondered why the British guards didn't try to shoot at them. They gathered their courage and moved even closer. Now they understood. Those "guards" were just dummies filled with straw!

Down in the harbor the British ships were raising their sails. One by one the ships turned their backs on Boston and sailed away. The Redcoats had decided not to fight. They were leaving Boston to the Americans!

The American soldiers were very excited. They swarmed into Boston. The people of the city greeted them with cheers of joy.

George Washington was happy, too. But he knew that he would not have long to enjoy his victory. The British weren't giving up on the war completely. Their big ships would be sure to show up again—and in some other city where the Americans were not so well prepared to fight back.

Washington knew now that the war would not be over any time soon. His letters were filled with gloomy predictions. "We expect a very bloody summer . . ." he wrote.

Washington guessed that the British were heading for New York. So he made sure that his army got there first.

The American soldiers reached New York on April 13. What they found did not make them very happy. Not everyone in the colonies was in favor of the war. Boston was a stronghold of the Patriots, as the American side was called. That was one reason why the British had been so quick to leave. In other parts of the colonies there were more people who did not support the war. Some were loyal to the English king; many others just wanted to stay out of trouble. In New York quite a few people had taken the British side. There was even a gilded statue of King George III in one of the city squares.

New York's location was another problem. Its broad rivers and deep harbor would be perfect for the British ships.

In June the British navy finally showed up. They docked their great ships near Staten Island, six miles south of the city. Then they waited. The Americans were left to wonder where and when the British would strike.

Washington decided that he would have to divide up his army. He sent one part of the army across the river to Brooklyn. In those days Brooklyn was just a tiny village. The rest of what is now a big city was covered with woods and marshes and a few little farms.

Toward the end of August the British finally started to move. British soldiers rowed across the harbor to Brooklyn and waded ashore through the marshes. Washington knew a big battle was brewing. But he still felt bold and confident.

Just before dawn on August 27 five American scouts were riding along a dirt road several miles from the waterfront. Suddenly they sensed that there were a lot of people nearby. Peering through the darkness they could make out a sea of brightly colored uniforms—red, green, and blue. The red uniforms belonged to the regular British soldiers, the redcoats. The blue and green uniforms belonged to the Hessians, German soldiers who were fighting in the British army.

The American scouts knew then that their side had been tricked. Instead of crossing New York Harbor from Staten Island, these soldiers had landed on the southern shore of Brooklyn and camped in the woods. They were going to take the Americans by surprise.

The scouts tried to turn back. But it was too late. British sentries had already seen them. They were dragged down from their horses and taken as prisoners.

At sunrise the scouts watched helplessly as the British broke camp and began their march. There were ten thousand enemy soldiers!

The Battle of Long Island began that day. Many of the Americans fought bravely. Some companies stayed put and fought even though they knew they would be killed. But most of the Patriot army decided to save their lives. They turned and ran. They didn't stop running until they reached the East River.

Washington was angry with his men for running away. But nothing the Americans did would have stopped the British. Two days later the Americans loaded their gear into their boats and sneaked across the river.

It was the first of many retreats.

That autumn the British chased the Americans into a fort that stood at the northern end of Manhattan Island. Then, in November, they chased them across the Hudson River and into New Jersey. By Christmastime the Americans had retreated all the way to Pennsylvania.

Many people thought the war was almost over. Congress fled from Philadelphia to

Baltimore. Some of the volunteer soldiers in the American army were getting ready to head for home. Others were talking about going over to the British side. The Americans even had trouble buying food. Farmers in Pennsylvania didn't want to take the paper money issued by Congress. They were afraid that the British would win and the money would be worthless before they had a chance to spend it.

General Washington still had faith in the cause. But he knew that something would have to happen soon to raise the spirits of the Patriot army. The soldiers desperately needed a victory.

Crossing the Delaware

CHRISTMAS NIGHT, 1776, ENDED WITH AN awful storm. First it rained. Then it snowed. Then hailstones the size of marbles came pelting down.

Through the worst of the weather the American army was on the move. All evening long, empty barges had been coming down the Delaware River to a place called McConkey's Ferry. The barge pilots picked up the soldiers who were waiting on the Pennsylvania side of the river. Then they used long poles to push the heavy boats across to the other bank.

Big blocks of ice were floating on the water. Sometimes they hit against the sides of the barges, almost swamping them. The snow came down so hard that it was impossible to see the far bank.

The soldiers' clothes got wet and froze solid. Soon the men felt as if they were wearing suits of ice.

General Washington was in one of the first boats. He made it across safely, but nothing else was going right. He had been counting on getting his whole army to the New Jersey side by midnight. Then they would sneak up on the enemy while they were asleep.

The storm slowed everything down. Now the sun was coming up, and the last boatloads were still being ferried across the water. "This made me despair of surprizing the Town," Washington wrote in his diary.

By the first light of dawn, December 26, Washington saw a strange sight. The rain had frozen on the trees, turning the branches into giant icicles. The road was slick with ice, too. It was the worst possible weather for marching. But it was too late to turn back. So the American army went slipping and sliding down the road.

For once, they were very lucky.

The Hessian soldiers had spent a comfortable Christmas in Trenton, New Jersey. Their commander did not think much of the Americans. One of his men had warned him to be ready for a battle, but he paid no attention. "Those country clowns cannot whip us!" he had bragged.

On Christmas night he had let his soldiers stay up celebrating. The next morning they were allowed to sleep late. When the American guns started to fire, the Hessians jumped out of bed. They ran outside, but they couldn't see much. It had started to snow again, and the snow was blowing right into the Hessians' eyes. Some of them were so confused, they ran around in circles.

After a little while the Hessian officers gave up trying to restore order. Someone went to the flagpole and pulled down the British flag.

The American soldiers could hardly believe their eyes. "The colors are down!" someone shouted. It was almost too good to be true.

"This," said Washington, "is a glorious day for our country."

After the fight at Trenton the British began to have some respect for George Washington. One British general called Washington "the Old Fox." Just when he seemed to be caught, Washington always had one more trick to play on the enemy.

But Washington's troubles were far from over.

Most of the American soldiers were volunteers. When many of them signed up, they had promised to stay in the army only until the end of 1776. Now their time in uniform was almost over. They were eager to get home to their families. A few days after his big victory, Washington was about to lose most of his army.

Two days before New Year's Washington rode out to talk to the volunteers. He called them together in a big field. He sat on his fine big horse and made a speech. At the end of it he promised to pay ten dollars to every soldier who stayed on for another six weeks. Ten dollars was not a great deal of money even then. But it was worth a lot more than today. Most of the soldiers would have a hard time earning ten dollars in six weeks.

George asked anyone who was willing to stay to step forward. The drummers played a tattoo on their drums: *Rat-a-tat-tat . . . Rat-a-tat-tat.*

But not a single man stepped forward.

Washington's heart was ready to break.

He rode a little closer and made another speech. "My brave fellows, you have done all that I asked you to do," he said. "But your country is at stake." This time he asked the men to stay, not for money, but for the sake of their cause. This present crisis will decide our destiny, he told them.

The drummers played again: *Rat-a-tat-tat . . . Rat-a-tat-tat.*

At first no one moved. Finally one man shrugged his shoulders and stepped out in front of the line. Then another. And another. Soon every man who was not wounded had come forward.

The Patriot army seemed to be making progress at last. They started to make their way across New Jersey, pushing the British back toward New York. But the British had a whole fleet of warships, and that gave them a big advantage. When summer came, General Howe sailed out of New York and headed up the Chesapeake Bay. Soon his soldiers marched into Philadelphia.

The American Congress had relocated to Baltimore. But Washington and his army were still just a few miles outside Philadelphia, not far from where they had been the winter before.

And this winter at Valley Forge, they were worse off than ever.

The soldiers were so hungry that they picked leaves off trees and bushes and tried to make soup from them! Their clothes were in shreds. Many of them had no shoes. They wrapped their feet in rags and tree bark to keep their toes from freezing. The barefoot soldiers left bloody footprints in the snow.

When General Washington walked through the camp, the hungry soldiers called out to him. "No meat!" they wailed. "No bread!" The chorus followed him everywhere he went. "No meat! No bread! No meat! No bread!" He couldn't get it out of his mind.

If the soldiers were going to keep from freezing, they would have to build their own huts. This was a problem. The men were already so cold and hungry that they were too weak to work. Washington offered a prize of twelve dollars to the group that built its hut fastest. Since there was a shortage of lumber, he also offered to pay one hundred dollars to anyone who could think of a substitute. But no one could think of a better way to build huts than with lumber.

Washington kept writing to Congress, begging for food and supplies. Finally a big shipment of shoes arrived from France. The soldiers rushed to unpack them. They were thrilled. Then their hearts sank. The French shoes were too small for the Americans' feet.

In the meantime, General Howe was less than twenty miles away. Everyone knew that he could march his army out of Philadelphia any time he wanted to and destroy Washington's camp. That would surely be the end of the American Revolution. But luckily for the Patriots, Howe was in no hurry. He had "the Old Fox" just where he wanted him. Howe seemed to think he could finish off Washington's army any time he felt like it.

Just when it seemed that things could not get worse, the Americans' perseverance began to pay off.

Even though everything seemed to be going General Howe's way, the British commander was getting discouraged. When he marched into Philadelphia, he had expected to be welcomed as a hero. But nothing of the kind happened. A few families who were against the war were happy to spend the winter partying with the British officers. Still, General Howe could see that the Patriots were not about to give up anytime soon. He got so discouraged that he decided to resign and go home to England.

Across the Atlantic the King of France had come to the same conclusion as General Howe. The French had been thinking about joining the fighting against England for some time. When spring came, and they were convinced that the Americans were not going to give up, they finally made their decision. France announced that it was sending a fleet of ships to America.

When Washington and his officers heard the news, they were so happy that they got up from the dinner table and danced around the room. "Long live the King of France!" someone shouted. "And long live our glorious cause!"

West Point

AT LONG LAST THE AMERICANS WERE hopeful. The new British commander, General Clinton, decided to give up Philadelphia and retreat to New York. But after that the war became a stalemate—neither side could figure out a way to win.

In the summer of 1780 the French ships finally arrived. Washington traveled from Pennsylvania to Connecticut to meet the French commander, whose name was Rochambeau. The Frenchman promised that there were more ships on the way. It was just a matter of time.

"Time," wrote Washington, "is precious beyond description." But there was nothing he could do but be patient.

After the meeting Washington and his aide, Alexander Hamilton, started back toward Pennsylvania. It was a long journey for two men on horseback. But Washington promised himself a treat. He was looking forward to visiting West Point, the largest and strongest of the American forts.

West Point stood on a cliff, just north of New York City. Its great guns pointed down on the Hudson River. The Americans had strung a big iron chain across the river. The chain was strong enough to keep the British ships from coming any farther north.

Washington was a good friend of the fort's commander, Benedict Arnold, and his pretty wife, Peggy. And when he reached their house a few miles above the fort, he was looking forward to a friendly visit.

But to his surprise neither of the Arnolds was there to meet him. General Arnold had been called to the fort on important business, an officer told Washington. Mrs. Arnold was still in bed.

Washington thought it was strange that Peggy Arnold didn't get up to greet her guests, but he was too polite to complain. So he and Hamilton ate breakfast alone. Then they went to visit some smaller forts nearby. When they returned to the house, it was three o'clock in the afternoon and the Arnolds still did not appear.

Dinnertime came, and it seemed that the general and his aide would be eating alone again. By now Washington was sure that something strange was going on.

General Washington went to his room to change for dinner. He was wondering what to do, when Alexander Hamilton came to the door, looking very excited. Hamilton had terrible news: A British spy named John André had been arrested that morning. And his captors had found maps of the fortress of West Point tucked into his boot!

Washington knew immediately what this meant. General Arnold had been scheming to betray West Point to the British. He was the one who had given André the maps!

Now the mystery of why Arnold hadn't shown up that day was solved. He had found out about André's arrest and run away. But where was Peggy Arnold?

Washington discovered that she had been in her room all day long! When he went to see her, she did not seem to recognize him. That's not General Washington, she shouted, that's the man who has come to kill my baby!

Washington insisted that he was not going to hurt anyone. But Mrs. Arnold seemed to have lost her mind. She began to cry and scream and say crazy things: Evil spirits were burning her head with a hot iron. They had burned her husband, too!

Washington felt very sorry for Mrs. Arnold. He was sure her husband's crime had driven her out of her mind. Or had it?

After she learned that General Arnold had made a safe escape, Peggy Arnold stopped talking about evil spirits. Suddenly her mind was normal again. Probably she had just been acting all along, even though no one could prove it.

Washington was happy that West Point had been saved. The morning after André's capture, Washington sat down and wrote a letter to Congress, telling them the whole story. The Americans who caught André, he said, had been offered "a large sum of Money" to let him escape. But they refused the bribe. Thanks to a few honest men, the American cause had been saved.

Even with help from the French, ending the

war was not easy.

Finally, in the fall of 1781, "the Old Fox" George Washington played his last trick. General Clinton and some of the British soldiers were in New York City. Another part of his army was in Virginia. Washington pretended that he was getting ready to surround New York. He sent carpenters to build the kinds of huts that soldiers used in the winter. He sent masons to build the big brick ovens that the army used for baking bread. He even wrote a letter, outlining a plan for attacking New York City. Then Washington made sure that the letter fell into the hands of a British spy.

In the meantime, the American army was hurrying down to Virginia. And the French ships were sailing south to meet them. By the time General Clinton caught on, it was too late. The British soldiers in Virginia were trapped near Yorktown.

On October 19, 1781, the British surrendered. The Americans could hardly believe that they were victorious at last. Everyone seemed surprised except Washington. "The work is done and well done," he said.

A New Nation

WHEN THE BRITISH SIGNED A TRUCE AT Yorktown, the band played a popular song called "The World Turned Upside Down." Everyone felt that this was just what had happened. The "raggedy" Americans had beaten the greatest army in the world!

But what now?

All during the war Washington had believed that the Americans were fighting for the right to found a new country. He even knew what that country ought to be called: The United States.

But not everyone had as much faith in this idea as General Washington did. Almost as soon as the British were defeated, the thirteen states started to fight among themselves. New York farmers and New Jersey farmers started to argue about who had the right to sell food to New York City. Connecticut and Pennsylvania fought over territory. They were so angry with each other that they almost went to war.

In the western part of Massachusetts, some farmers decided that they did not like paying taxes to Boston any more than they liked paying them to the British. First, eastern Massachusetts sent an army to western Massachusetts to fight the rebel farmers. Then Rhode Island said the rebels were welcome to come and live there. So all the other states were upset with Rhode Island.

A few people said that the American states should find a king to come and rule over them. Only a king would be strong enough to keep the colonies from quarreling among themselves.

Others did not want the colonies to be united at all. They were afraid that the freedom they fought so hard for would be taken away from them.

Washington did not want any part of these new quarrels. When he left Mount Vernon to head the army in 1775, he had expected the war to be over in a matter of months. Instead, he had been away from home for six long years. Now he just wanted to go home.

Even so, two more years passed before the peace treaty was signed. Washington stayed with the army until December of 1783. Then he said good-bye to the officers who had been with him for so long.

Washington was only fifty-two years old when he left the army. But he felt like an old man. "I have grown both blind and grey in your service," he told one group of officers.

He wore thick glasses. His hearing was bad. His teeth had fallen out, and his false teeth pinched his gums. All he wanted was to go back home to Mount Vernon and be a farmer again.

For a while that is just what he did. Martha Washington's son, Jack, had caught a fever and died during the war. George and Martha decided to adopt two of Jack's children. Once again there were children at Mount Vernon. They ran through the halls and rode horseback across the fields. When a friend wrote Washington to ask how he was doing, he wrote back that he was "gliding down the stream of life."

Even though he was retired, he was still the most famous man in America. Almost every day visitors showed up at Mount Vernon. Many of the visitors wanted favors. Quite a few ended up asking to borrow money. Other admirers sent him presents. Some were beautiful and valuable. Others were just unusual. The king of Spain sent Washington a jackass. Washington named it Royal Gift.

In the summer of 1787 the colonies decided to try one more time to settle their differences. They held a convention in Philadelphia to discuss a Constitution—a written plan for a new government.

Virginia asked George Washington to be part of its delegation. And when he arrived, he was elected president of the entire convention. For months he sat in the chair of honor in the front of the hall and listened to the other delegates argue. Everyone wondered what Washington was thinking.

Finally the delegates came up with a plan for the Constitution. But would it pass?

At the last minute Washington let it be known that he was planning to vote yes. His decision had a big influence on other delegates, and the Constitution was adopted.

When it came time to pick the first President of the new country, once again everyone thought of George Washington. Every state had its heroes, but Washington was the only American hero whose name was known in all of the new states—and in other countries as well.

The trouble was, Washington was not sure he wanted to be president. Strangely enough, this only made everyone more convinced that he was ideal for the job. In all the years that he led the army, Washington had never accepted a single dollar in pay. What's more, he hadn't made enemies by getting too involved in the states' quarrels with one another. Everyone trusted Washington to be more interested in the good of the country than in money or personal power.

Our First President

"LONG LIVE WASHINGTON!" SHOUTED THE crowds. "God bless our President!"

George Washington stood on the steps of Federal Hall in New York City and looked out at the sea of happy faces. Thousands of people had filled the streets to see him take his oath as the new nation's first president. They cheered so hard, it seemed as if they would never stop. And over the cheering Washington could hear the sound of cannons, booming out a thirteen-gun salute.

Washington had never been so popular. He had come from Mount Vernon in a horse-drawn carriage, and along the way crowds turned out to wave at the carriage and throw flowers. At every stop he had been invited to be the guest of honor at a banquet. He joked that it was almost as if the people expected him to eat his way into office.

It seemed that the new president could do

no wrong. People called him "Your Excellency" and "Your Highness." Some people even called him "Your Majesty." They called Martha "Lady Washington."

Martha Washington did not enjoy all the fuss that was made over her and her husband. When she and the president took a home in Philadelphia, where the government had moved after some months in New York, she found she couldn't go outside without attracting a crowd. Her days were filled with official tea parties and dinners. She complained that the parties were "very dull."

So many people came to meet the president that they wore out the furniture. Mrs. Washington was kept busy ordering new chairs and carpets.

But the new president's popularity did not last long.

During Washington's time in office the United States faced one crisis after another. First, members of Washington's cabinet quarreled bitterly over how the new government should be set up and who would have the power. Out on the frontier, near the Forks of the Ohio, where Washington had traveled as a young man, there were still some farmers who did not want to pay taxes to the new government.

The worst troubles began when England and France started fighting each other again. Washington did not want to get involved. He was afraid that the United States was not strong enough to survive another war. But many Americans thought we ought to help France. After all, the French had come to our aid during the Revolution.

Suddenly the president was no longer a hero. Instead of cheering him, crowds marched through the streets calling him names. At night they gathered in front of his house, waving fiery torches. When Washington looked out of his window, they greeted him with boos and catcalls.

In spite of these troubles, Washington worked very hard. He traveled around the new country, giving as many people as possible a chance to see and talk to their leader. He tried to settle the arguments among his cabinet members in a way that would keep the country strong.

One job Washington especially enjoyed was the planning of a brand-new capital, to be called Federal City. First he chose a plot of land that was near his beloved home, Mount Vernon. Then he hired a French architect named Pierre L'Enfant to draw up a plan.

L'Enfant imagined a dignified capital city that would someday grow to be very large. There would be broad avenues and plenty of space for grand buildings and public monuments. When L'Enfant described his ideas, some people laughed at him. The government would never need such big buildings, they said. Surely there would never be enough traffic to fill up those wide streets!

Thomas Jefferson, another Virginia politician, disliked L'Enfant so much that he managed to get him fired. Washington refused to throw out the plan along with its creator. Work on Federal City went forward, but his critics thought this was just another of the president's mistakes.

After two terms as president George Washington decided to retire. Like so many of his decisions, this one caused an uproar. Many people thought a president should keep on being re-elected until he died in office. They argued that choosing a new leader every four years, or even every eight, would tear the country apart.

President Washington had more faith in the future. He sent the newspapers a message saying good-bye and giving his final advice to his countrymen. The message urged Americans to look to the Constitution to keep the United States strong and independent. Then he sat back and let the election for the second president go ahead.

In the spring of 1797 the Washingtons returned home for good. Like any family, they had their problems on moving day. They had too much furniture to move by wagon, so they had to hire a boat to take most of the furniture up the Potomac River to Mount Vernon. Even so, their coach was stuffed full. The Washingtons sat crowded in among the boxes and packing cases. Martha's little dog jumped into the coach and curled up at their feet. Then, at the last minute, someone remembered the pet parrot.

Washington grumbled that he would have been just as happy if the dog and parrot were "both forgot." But of course he moved over to make room for them. Finally everything was ready, and the coach took to the road.

George Washington thought he had been a failure as president. For years people had criticized every move he made. But as the coach made its way to Virginia, the Washingtons found they still had many friends. In many towns the leading citizens rode out on horseback to act as an escort. Farm families and villagers lined the road to wave as the coach passed by. The crowds were not as big and noisy as they had been eight years before, but this time there were tears in the people's eyes.

Mount Vernon Again

DURING THE EIGHT YEARS HE HAD BEEN away, Mount Vernon had become very run down. The house was in such bad repair that Washington was afraid to invite guests to dinner. He thought that if a large group sat down in the dining room, the floor might collapse and dump them all into the cellar.

Once again he got up every morning at dawn. It was going to take a lot of work to make Mount Vernon a home again.

He was so busy that when he caught a bad cold, he did not want to take time off. He had caught colds before, and sooner or later they always went away. But this time the cold did not go away. Washington's throat got so sore and swollen that he could hardly breathe. Finally the doctors were called in, but they did not know what to do. Two days later George Washington died. The date was December 14, 1799.

Sad as Washington's death was, many

people felt that the date of his death was symbolic. The United States was about to enter a new century—the 1800s. Washington and his life's work belonged to the old century. He would always be remembered as the Father of his Country. But now the country was ready to start growing up.

All his life George Washington was a shy hero. When he died, he left behind strict instructions. There was to be no big public funeral. No parades. No flowery speeches. And no crowds. Washington asked to be buried at Mount Vernon, on a grassy hillside overlooking the river.

But Washington's modesty made him more of a hero than ever in the eyes of his countrymen. Almost as soon as Washington retired, people had started to realize how special he was. The colonists who rebelled against Britain had been very lucky to find a strong leader who was not greedy for power.

Over the years many monuments to George Washington were established. Some statues showed him dressed as an ancient Roman, bare-chested except for a toga slung

over one shoulder. Books were published
containing made-up "facts" about his life—
such as the story that as a boy he chopped
down a cherry tree and then confessed to his
father, saying "I cannot tell a lie." Washington had been famous for so long, that few
people remembered what he had been like as
a young man—the awkward, redheaded
youth who camped on the bank of the Ohio
and dreamed of the day when the wilderness
would be transformed into a land of fertile
farms and prosperous cities and towns.

George Washington did receive one trib-
ute that was very fitting. In 1791 Congress
voted to change the name of the new capital
city that was going up on the banks of the
Potomac River. The capital would no longer
be called Federal City. From then on its
name would be Washington. Over the years
Americans came to see that Washington's
idea of what the new city could be had been
right after all. The great city of Washington,
D. C., became a living memorial to our first
president's vision.

Highlights in the Life of
GEORGE WASHINGTON

1732 On February 22, George Washington is born in Virginia.

1753 On October 31, Washington leaves Virginia on an important mission for Governor Dinwiddie.

1754 In April, Washington leads an expedition of one hundred and fifty Virginians to fight the French.

In May, Washington is promoted to colonel and is in charge of all the Virginia volunteers. But he loses his first battle with the French at Fort Necessity on July 3.

1755 Washington returns to fight the French as an aide to General Braddock.

1759 On January 6, George marries Martha Dandridge Custis.

1774 In the fall, Washington attends the First Continental Congress as a delegate from Virginia.

1775 On June 16, Washington is appointed commander of the American army.

1776 On July 4, the Declaration of Independence is adopted, and the United States is born.

1777   The Americans set up their winter camp at Valley Forge.

1780   On September 25, Washington discovers Benedict Arnold's plot to betray West Point to the British.

1781   The American army and the French fleet trap the British at Yorktown, Virginia. On October 19, the British surrender. The war has been won.

1787   In May, Washington is elected president of the Constitutional Convention. On September 17, the delegates approve the Constitution.

1789   Washington is elected president of the United States on February 4. He takes the oath of office in New York on April 30.

1793   Washington begins his second term as president.

On September 18, he lays the cornerstone for the Capitol building in Washington, D.C.

1799   Washington dies on December 14.

For Further Study

More Books to Read

The Founding Fathers. Bennett Wayne (Garrard)

George Washington. Keith Brandt (Troll Associates)

George Washington. Tom McGovern (Watts)

George Washington and the Birth of Our Nation. Milton Meltzer (Watts)

George Washington: Father of Freedom. Stewart Graff (Chelsea House)

George Washington: Young Leader. Laurence Santrey (Troll Associates)

George Washington: Young Leader. Augusta Stevenson (Macmillan)

George Washington's Breakfast. Jean Fritz (Putnam)

If You Grew Up With George Washington. Ruth B. Gross (Scholastic)

Valley Forge. Libby Hughes (Macmillan)

Washington. William Jacobs (Macmillan)

The Washington Way. Morris Jeffrey (Lerner)

The World of Young George Washington. Suzanne Hilton (Walker)

Videos

George Washington. (Coronet/The Multimedia Co.)

George Washington. (SECAM)

George Washington. (Spoken Arts)

Meet George Washington. (Zenger Video)

Index

United States 80, 81, 88, 89, 91, 94

Valley Forge 71
van Braam, Jacob 22
Virginia 9, 11, 13, 15, 19, 20, 21, 23, 26, 28, 31, 32, 33, 34, 35, 36, 38, 43, 47, 52, 79, 83, 92
Virginia "volunteers" 33
Virginians 9, 21, 23, 26, 28, 31, 32, 35, 36, 38

Washington, Augustine (father) 8, 12
Washington, Augustine (half brother) 8, 12
Washington, D. C. 95
Washington, Jack (brother) 34

Washington, Lawrence (half brother) 7, 8, 9, 10, 11, 12, 13, 14, 18, 19, 20, 43
Washington, Martha Custis Dandridge (wife) 42, 43, 45, 46, 47, 48, 82, 88, 91
Washington, Mary (mother) 8, 12, 14, 15
West Point 74, 75, 76, 78
Williamsburg (Virginia) 32

"Yankee Doodle" 51
Yorktown 79, 80